For

Copyright © 1997
Peter Pauper Press, Inc.
202 Mamaroneck Avenue
White Plains, NY 10601
All rights reserved.
ISBN 0-88088-115-1
Printed in Singapore
7 6 5 4 3 2 1

To Grandma

With Love

*Original text by Claudine Gandolfi
Compiled by Esther L. Beilenson
and Claudine Gandolfi*

*Cover Illustration by Judith Sutton
Design by Lesley Ehlers*

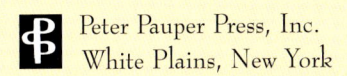

Peter Pauper Press, Inc.
White Plains, New York

Contents

Introduction * 7

We Have Become a Grandmother * 8

Memories Are Made of This * 17

Grandma's Love * 31

Grandma Is with You Always * 43

The Best Club in the World * 52

Introduction

Grandmother and grandchildren. There is so much love and joy on both sides. It's a very special relationship indeed, and not just because they have a common enemy—the parents! On the grandmother's side, it is pure love, given with the knowledge that the feeling will be returned unconditionally. On the grandchild's part, it is pure joy, the enjoyment of a very special adult who gives all of herself but invokes none of the usual rules. In the pages that follow, you're sure to find great pleasure while exploring this special relationship.

C. G. and E. L. B.

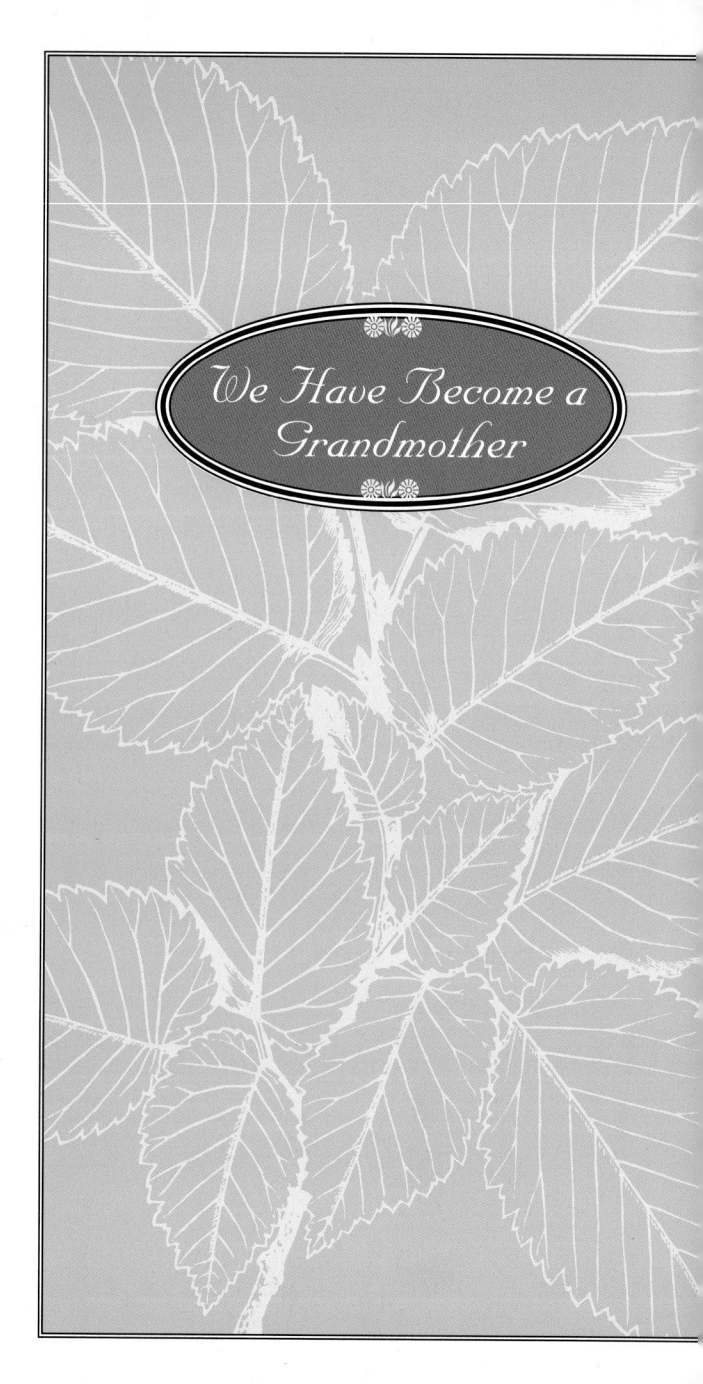

We Have Become a Grandmother

To Grandma,

   Mom, this is just a little note to let you know that you are now a card-carrying grandma! So, you'd best clean out the photo section in your wallet.

   That's right, after nine months of anticipation, the blessed event finally occurred. I'm sorry you couldn't be here to share this with me but, even so, I'm glad that everything else turned out fine.

   Michael and I will be coming for a visit with the baby as soon as possible. She has blue eyes and curly strawberry blonde hair, just like her grandma.

Your loving daughter,
Catherine

PS: We named her Emily, after you!

We have become a grandmother.
>   Margaret Thatcher

We never know of the love of our parents for us till we have become parents.
>   Henry Ward Beecher

By some miracle the daughter she complains about (you) gives birth to the Perfect Grandchild!
>   Ellen Sue Stern

You feel completely comfortable entrusting your baby to them for long periods of time, which is why most grandparents flee to Florida at the earliest opportunity.
>   Dave Barry

If you would civilize a man, begin with his grandmother.
>   Victor Hugo

I feel enthusiastic to be a grandmother. It's a rejuvenating experience. I wish my children had had children sooner.

         Anonymous

It has often been pointed out that some deeply emotional family bonds sometimes seem to skip a generation. There is so much mundane detail between parent and child—and frequently so much tension, so much obligation and unspoken expectations—that the relationship between child and grandparent takes on a special significance.

      Dr. Ruth Westheimer,
      The Value of Family

Our mothers and grandmothers, some of them: moving to music not yet written.

         Alice Walker

$\mathcal{Y}$ou will never really know what kind of parent you were or if you did it right or wrong. And you will worry about this and them as long as you live. But when your children have children and you watch them do what they do, you will have part of an answer.
Robert Fulghum

$\mathcal{A}$ mother becomes a true grandmother the day she stops noticing the terrible things her children do because she is so enchanted with the wonderful things her grandchildren do.
Lois Wyse

$\mathcal{I}$t is as grandmothers that mothers come into the fullness of their grace.
Christopher Morley

$\mathcal{G}$randparents are our continuing tie to the near-past, to the events and beliefs and experiences that so strongly affect our lives and the world around us.

Jimmy Carter

I am joyful because I have four children whom I love and who love me. I believe that my children, their partners and their children, are the most precious things in the world.

Ann Tuite

Grandparenting is unlike any experience life has offered before. It is like a day at the beach without sunburn, a picnic without ants, or income without taxation. Grandparenting is a job that we can tailor to our own specific style and talents.

*C. Ciardi, C. Orme, C. Quatrano,
The Magic of Grandparenting*

If I had known my grandchildren were going to be so wonderful, I would have had more children!

Lois L. Kaufman

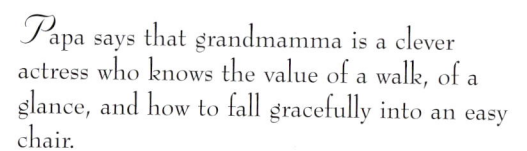

Papa says that grandmamma is a clever actress who knows the value of a walk, of a glance, and how to fall gracefully into an easy chair.

Honoré de Balzac

When a woman gets ready to become a grandmother, she begins developing a few of those charming peculiarities of which grandmotherhood is wrought. Even if she were formerly vice-president for actuarial services at her company, she suddenly begins keeping llamas in her kitchen.

Colin McEnroe

My mother became a different person when she graduated into the magic realm of grandmotherdom, where she reigned as both healer and cheerleader. She threw out all the rule books and suspended judgment and impatience. There were no strings attached to her love.

Alexandra Stoddard

Perfect love sometimes does not come until the first grandchild.
>	Welsh Proverb

A grandmother will put a sweater on you when she is cold, feed you when she is hungry and put you to bed when she is tired.
>	Erma Bombeck

Becoming a grandparent is a second chance, for you have a chance to put to use all the things you learned the first time. It's all love and no discipline.
>	Dr. Joyce Brothers

Grandparents are frequently more congenial with their grandchildren than with their children.
>	André Maurois

I suddenly realized that through no act of my own I had become biologically related to a new human being.

Margaret Mead

*G*randmotherhood will transform your mother from a responsible type into a fun fanatic.

Colin McEnroe

*W*hen a child is born, so are grandmothers.

Judith Levy

*I*t doesn't seem possible that your baby can have a baby until she does it.

Eleanor Budoff

A home without a grandmother is like an egg without salt.

Florence King

Memories Are Made of This

Dear Grandma,

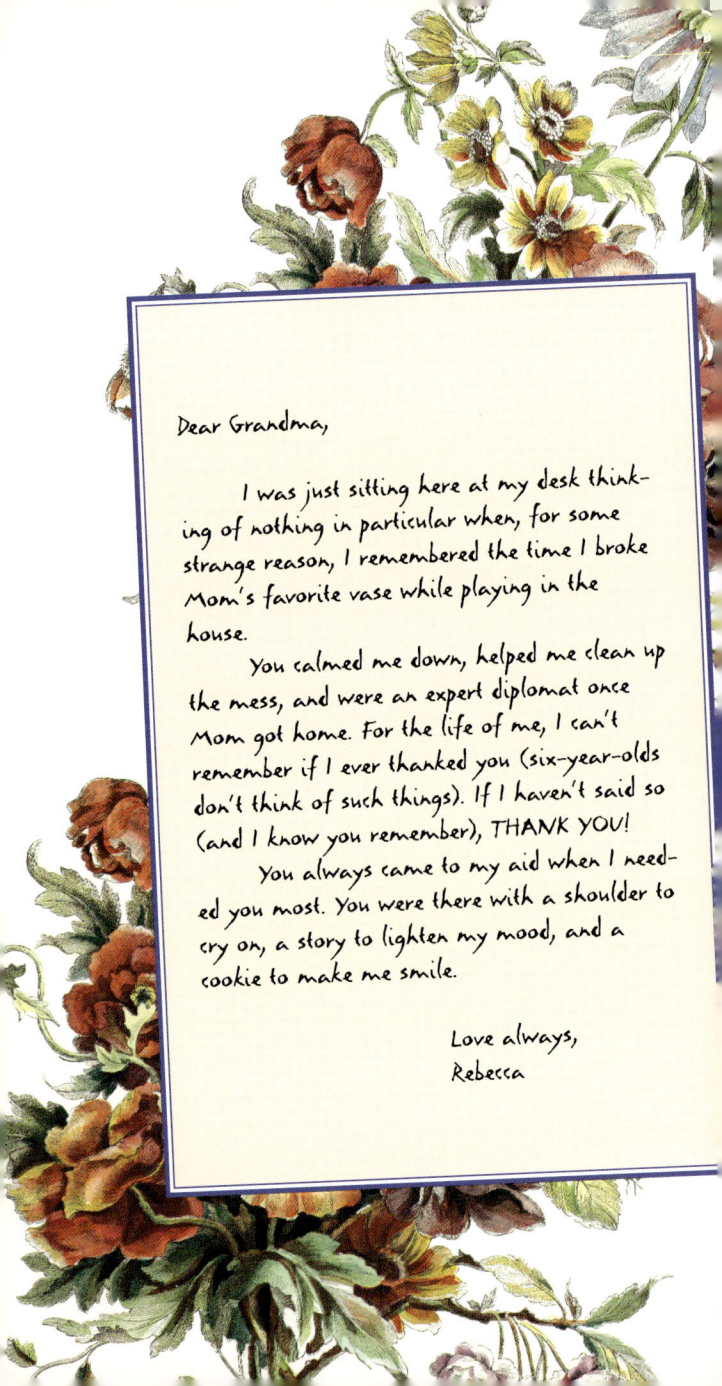

    I was just sitting here at my desk thinking of nothing in particular when, for some strange reason, I remembered the time I broke Mom's favorite vase while playing in the house.

    You calmed me down, helped me clean up the mess, and were an expert diplomat once Mom got home. For the life of me, I can't remember if I ever thanked you (six-year-olds don't think of such things). If I haven't said so (and I know you remember), THANK YOU!

    You always came to my aid when I needed you most. You were there with a shoulder to cry on, a story to lighten my mood, and a cookie to make me smile.

                      Love always,
                        Rebecca

When I think of my grandparents, I think of the silver candy dish on the walnut coffee table in their home. As children, each time my siblings and I visited our grandparents, we raced each other to the covered dish. And whenever we opened the lid, there was always something special inside. Though I am well past my childhood years, I will even admit to secretly peeking in the dish on my last visit.

Terri Harrison

[Grandmother] baked like a dream. . . . When she went to market, she always bought oranges and peppermint sticks for the children. She would cut a hole in an orange, insert a peppermint stick, and then we'd squeeze the orange and suck the juice through the stick. It was one of the best things I ever tasted.

Helen Hayes

If I really begged her, Nanny would take her teeth out and smile at me. I never saw anything so funny in my life. She kept them in a glass by the bed. She didn't wear them all the time because they were kind of loose and clicked around in her mouth. She'd run her tongue over the uppers to put them back in place.

Carol Burnett

[Grandmother Flora Belle] was just about the best midwife in Jamestown and was much in demand. Flora Belle was a dedicated nurse with a very open, welcoming attitude toward the world. Always cooking, cleaning, sewing. She was a sunny, active, vigorous woman, a dreamer and a planner. Nothing was too much for her, no hours too long, no time better spent than doing things for her family.

Lucille Ball

My grandmother was famous for her baking, and every day she served another marvel for dessert: shortbreads crowned with meringue, cinnamon-scented apple pie, golden strudel that only tasted light. One winter night in the depths of the Depression, when she had no meat or vegetables left, she thrilled my mother with a dinner made from cream, sugar, flour and copious quantities of butter whipped to lemony softness with a wooden spoon. It must have been murder on the arteries, but I'm told it did wonders for the soul.

Rona Maynard

I loved my grandparents' home. Everything smelled older, worn but safe; the food aroma had baked itself into the furniture.

Susan Strasberg

Grandma . . . would listen to our problems; pull our loose teeth with her pointed pliers; cut and curl our hair; rub Mentholatum on anything that was hurt, bruised, or broken; and threaten to sell us to the gypsies if we misbehaved. She sang songs I never heard before, whistled when she did the dishes, and recited old-fashioned poems. She taught me to believe in fairies and showed me where they lived.

Teresa Wendel

She read me the comics (I would correct her on her characterizations), and she sewed and made cakes and cookies, just like Grandma is supposed to.

David Carradine

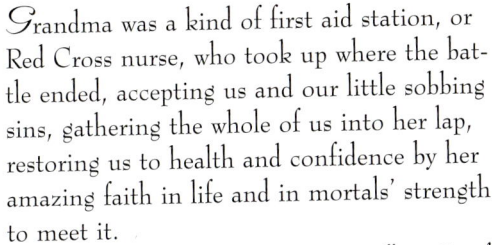

Grandma was a kind of first aid station, or Red Cross nurse, who took up where the battle ended, accepting us and our little sobbing sins, gathering the whole of us into her lap, restoring us to health and confidence by her amazing faith in life and in mortals' strength to meet it.

Lillian Smith

[My] Gramma Sally and Gramma Hazel . . . both lived for a long, long time. . . . They were a constant part of our lives, and not just at holidays and birthdays and funerals. They were part of my own daughter's childhood, part of the extended family that welcomed her and raised her. From them I learned about the wisdom of old age, about the importance of family—and about the power of matriarchs.

Loni Anderson

She would engage you in real conversation if she found you sitting alone at a party, or she would draw out of you what you wanted to do with your life and encourage you, particularly if your ambition involved leaving Boston or becoming some sort of artist.

Honor Moore,
on her grandmother Margarett Sargent

Now my grandmother was something else! She was adorable. After her husband's death, she ran the bakery, raised all those kids, and managed to enjoy her life.

Doris Day

What I remember most is her absolute personal integrity, her strong will, her work ethic, her soothing deep alto voice, and her gentle touch.

Robert C. Atchley

Grandma served as general homemaker for us all: cooking, mending, cleaning, shopping, and being my main bedtime storyteller.

Mary Tyler Moore

My grandmother did washing, and my mother and her sister went to a little one-room school. One day the teacher, who was about 16 and white, was doing long division and having trouble explaining it. Since my mother and her sister already knew long division, they explained it to her and the class. They came home all excited and proud of themselves, crowing, "Mama, guess what we did? We taught the teacher long division." My grandmother just said to her husband "Johnny, we have to move."

Toni Morrison

I never thought she'd turn on me. When I was sinking in a sea of diapers, formulas and congenital spitting, Mother couldn't wait to pull her grandchildren onto her lap and say, "Let me tell you how rotten your mommy was. She never took naps, and she never picked up her room, and she had a mouth like a drunken sailor in Shanghai."

Erma Bombeck

Nanny and I would go downtown to the main street where all the stores were and window-shop. She'd hold on to my hand real tight so she wouldn't lose me. She walked pretty fast, and when she'd spot a bargain, she'd get so excited and so scared that somebody might beat her to it I thought she was going to jerk my arm clear off my body and leave the rest of me there without ever turning around.

Carol Burnett

Granny [enjoyed] her brood in a true grandmotherly orgy; you climbed to the attic to play bandits, sneaked into the club to swim in the pool, and got decked out in my nightgowns to perform amateurish plays. In the company of that adorable woman, you . . . spent the summer baking cookies and the winter knitting striped mufflers for your friends.

Isabel Allende,
Paula

She was as tough and as lovable and as proper as a well-polished old army-boot. She had her sweet side and made great blueberry muffins and cherry pies. . . . It seemed to me that Granny Peck must have known every berry patch in Pennsylvania. She was also a great gardener. . . . She could make anything grow, no matter how dead it looked when she got hold of it.

David Carradine

Everyone adored her. She was witty and droll without even a hint of cynicism. Each of her grandchildren was absolutely certain that he or she was the most loved by Mammy.

Gangaji,
a.k.a. Antoinette Robinson Warner

A bunch of women from the First Baptist Church Ladies Auxiliary, as devout and arbitrary a bunch of women as you could hope to find in Cobb County, came to my grandmother's house for what appeared to be social reasons. . . . One of them said . . . "Judy, we understand that you are giving Carol's old clothes to the colored maid's girl and we think they are nice enough to give to one of the white girls over at the school." My grandmother's response was a less profane version of "Don't let the screen door hit you in the ass on the way out."

Brett Butler

My mom and grandmother became the most important people in my life. They taught me everything I would ever know about survival, pride, and character. They were my role models. . . . Not a single day passes when I don't think of [my grandmother's] words: "When it all comes down to the final day, you'll have to look in the mirror at yourself and God, and only then will you be judged." . . . My grandmother had a deep impact on me in more ways than one, but particularly when it comes to my faith in God.

Charles Barkley

My full name is Lois Maureen Stapleton. I never was known as Lois; the only person to call me that was my maternal grandmother, and she only used it when she was angry. I knew I'd done something wrong when I'd hear her cry out, "Lois Maureen, I want to talk to you."

Maureen Stapleton

Many of my memories of [my grandmother] are from childhood. But when I take out Nana's cookbook, read the notes written in her hand and take her advice on what to cook, she speaks to me again—not as grandmother to child, but as woman to woman, in the language she knew best.

Mary Taylor Gray

No question, our home was a classic matriarchy. My grandmother was never wrong. She owned us. I tell you, you really want to find out about my family, go talk to Grandma.

Gary David Goldberg

Children are like wet cement. Whatever falls on them makes an impression.

Haim Ginott

Grandma's Love

DEAR GRANDMA,

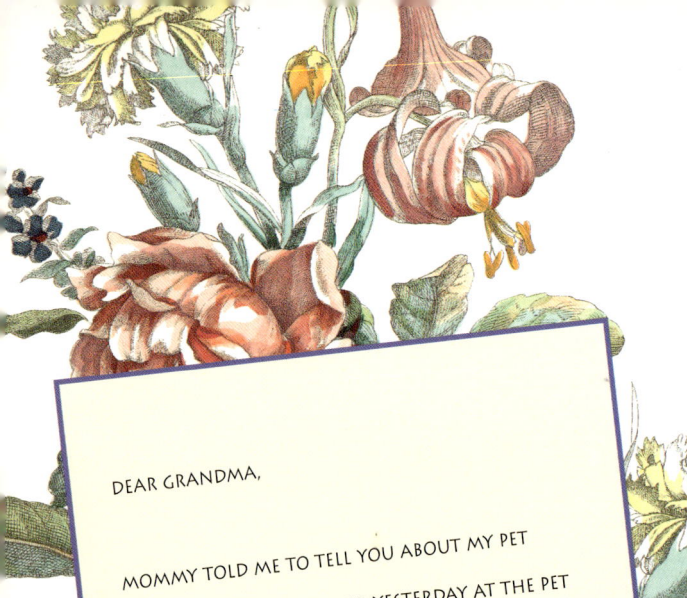

MOMMY TOLD ME TO TELL YOU ABOUT MY PET HAMSTER, FRED. I GOT FRED YESTERDAY AT THE PET SHOP BECAUSE MY TOOTH CAME OUT. IT ONLY HURT A LITTLE BIT. MOMMY SAID I WAS A VERY GOOD GIRL. SHE LET ME PICK FRED OUT OF A BUNCH OF HAMSTERS IN A BIG FISH TANK. HE IS BROWN WITH A WHITE PATCH ON HIS BELLY. HE IS VERY SOFT AND WARM AND I PLAY WITH HIM EVERY DAY. WHEN YOU VISIT, I WILL LET YOU PLAY WITH HIM. HE ONLY BITES A LITTLE BIT.

LOVE,

KELLY

As a granny, I follow rules the parents have established and within those boundaries I am free to love those kids to excess. I have never had any other relationship so completely free of emotional complications.

Sheila Kitzinger

My grandmother was 91 when my daughter was born. . . . I couldn't hear what my grandmother said to her only great-granddaughter, but I know what wish she would have bestowed, and I know my daughter. "You'll break their hearts," she must have said.

Kathryn Harrison

Her mother loved her dearly and so did her grandmother who doted on her with even greater tenderness.

Charles Perrault,
Little Red Riding Hood

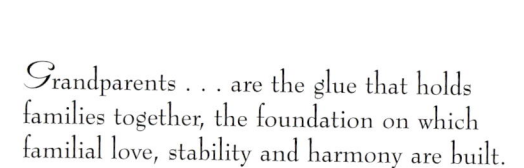

Grandparents . . . are the glue that holds families together, the foundation on which familial love, stability and harmony are built.
Ebony Magazine

She was such a wonderful person. All the children loved her. I was always proud of my grandmother because she cared for everyone. She always had a kind word for everyone. I never saw her upset or cross.
Sunceri Dawson

A child who has a grandparent has a softened view of the universe and knows that there is more to life than what we see, more than getting and gaining, winning and losing. There is a love that makes no demands.
Lois Wyse

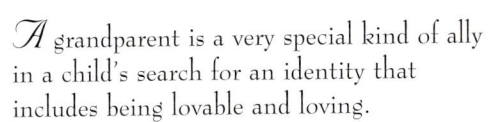

$\mathcal{A}$ grandparent is a very special kind of ally in a child's search for an identity that includes being lovable and loving.

> Fred Rogers,
> a.k.a. Mister Rogers

$\mathcal{A}$nd so our mothers and grandmothers have, more often than not anonymously, handed on the creative spark, the seed of the flower they themselves never hoped to see: or like a sealed letter they could not plainly read.

> Alice Walker

$\mathcal{L}$et's bring back grandmothers—the old-fashioned kind, who take you by the hand and lead you into the future, safe and savvy and smarter than your mother.

> Florence King

How much better off were the mothers, grandmothers and great-grandmothers who lived in extended families with extra arms to hug a needy child and extra ears to listen to her complaints!

Evelyn Bassoff

Grandmothers can offer our grandchildren unconditional love, be a source of their roots, and be heard in ways that our own children never hear us. If we choose, we can fill a need that can be filled by no one else. As has been said, we'll be remembered for the time (not the money) we give our grandchildren.

Vicki Lansky

I have never met anyone who had quite the amazing force without effort that my grandmother possessed.

Ethel Barrymore

We all know grandparents whose values transcend passing fads and pressures and who possess the wisdom of distilled pain and joy. Because they are usually free to love and guide and befriend the young without having to take daily responsibility for them, they can often reach out past pride and fear of failure and close the space between generations.

Jimmy Carter

The woman was a great mountain. Yes, it was she who led them out of the old world into the new one.

*Gertrude Stein,
on her grandmother Hannah Stein*

A grandmother's kiss can cure anything from a bump on the head to a broken heart.

Anonymous

No one . . . who has not known that inestimable privilege can possibly realize what good fortune it is to grow up in a home where there are grandparents.
Suzanne La Follette

Every family needs the love and input from grandma.
Louis Gossett, Jr.

Grandmothers are the ones children go to for love, for stories, for comfort when they've been scolded, for guidance, and, of course, for treats.
Mildred Bollinger Andrews

Who takes the child by the hand takes the mother by the heart.
German Proverb

My grandmother, Bobbe Mary, was the one adult I adored, because she encouraged my need to be the center of all creation.
Roseanne

Grandparents somehow sprinkle a sense of stardust over grandchildren.
Alex Haley

Grandma always said that it almost feels too good to be alive.
Anna Lee Walters

To Angela her grandmother was old but had not grown older and was never younger. This is a usual way with grandmothers.
Cynthia Propper Seton

The closest friends I have made all through life have been people who also grew up close to a loved and loving grandmother or grandfather.

Margaret Mead

In recent years I have made a habit to ask people about their grandparents. Almost universally, before they even begin to respond with words, a broad smile comes across their faces. That's the "Magic of Grandparenting." It is a legacy of the best kind of love because it is given with little, if any, thought to what the giver will get in return.

Cathryn Girard

It was Graddy Hayes who ran [our] household, providing for us, feeding us. . . . [She] was truly a remarkable woman, the strength of my young life.

Helen Hayes

I was an angel in her eyes, no matter what the facts were, no matter what anyone else happened to think.

Judy Langford Carter

My own grandmother was one of those unprofessional nurses who served without recompense, from the mere love of it. But you have had grandmothers of your own, you know how it went. You remember the old woman who nursed you when you had scarlet fever, and walked the floor with you when you had whooping cough. Money will never buy such attendance for you again.

Willa Cather

My grandmother was a good teacher, a dedicated teacher, but not a coddling teacher. She taught through a combination of cajolery, humiliation, and very occasional praise.

Michael Milton

Everyone called her Momma, and she was, indeed, the mother of us all.

> Maureen Stapleton,
> on her maternal grandmother

Going to see my grandparents was the highlight of my childhood summers. . . . I was doted upon, admired, entertained and overfed. I was never more content and happy.

> Carolyn Anthony

She loved children. She would give each child some form of special individual attention. It could be a smile, a pat, brushing a bit of hair out of a child's eyes, drying a tear, or just letting each one know that someone cared.

> Sunceri Dawson

Grandma Is with You Always

Dear Grandma,

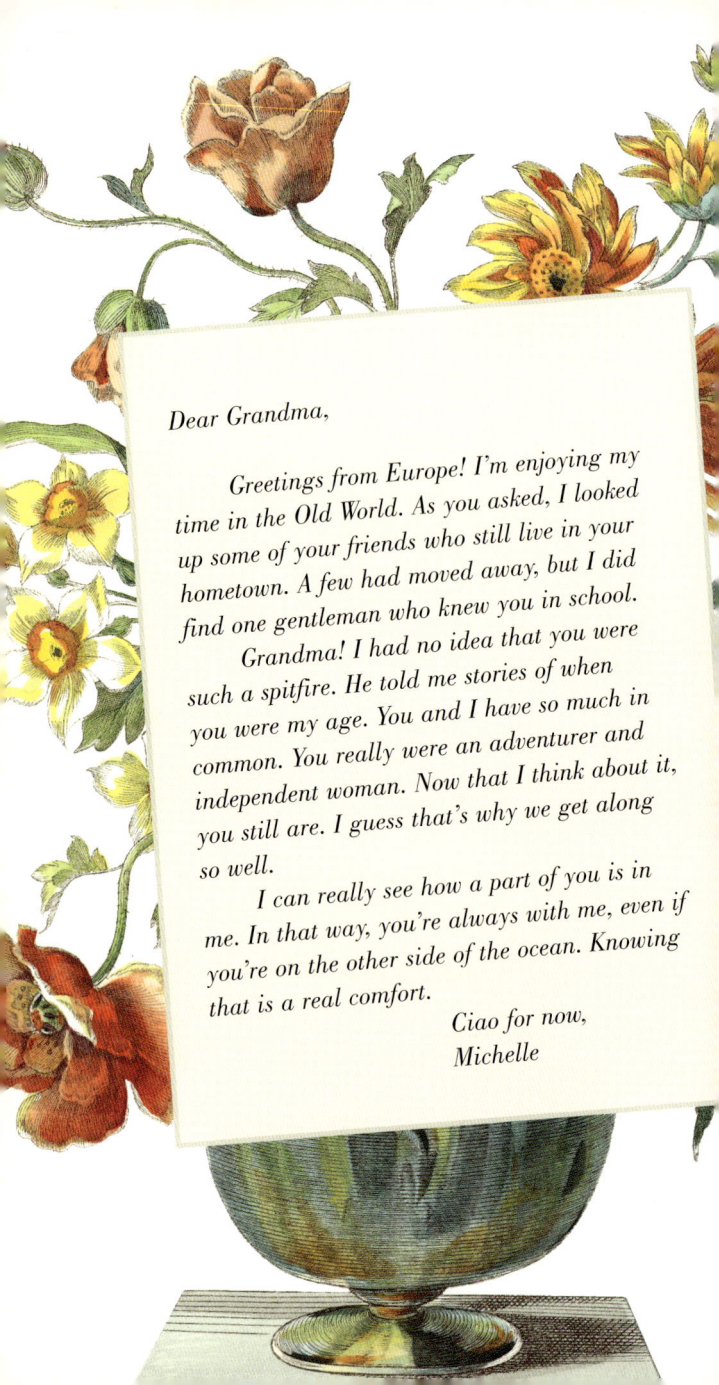

    Greetings from Europe! I'm enjoying my time in the Old World. As you asked, I looked up some of your friends who still live in your hometown. A few had moved away, but I did find one gentleman who knew you in school.

    Grandma! I had no idea that you were such a spitfire. He told me stories of when you were my age. You and I have so much in common. You really were an adventurer and independent woman. Now that I think about it, you still are. I guess that's why we get along so well.

    I can really see how a part of you is in me. In that way, you're always with me, even if you're on the other side of the ocean. Knowing that is a real comfort.

                    Ciao for now,
                      Michelle

The strength of my conscience came from Grandma, who meant what she said. Perhaps nothing is more valuable for a child than living with an adult who is firm and loving–and Grandma was loving.

Margaret Mead

It is one of nature's ways that we often feel closer to distant generations than to the generation immediately preceding us.

Igor Stravinsky

Nothing makes a boy smarter than being a grandson.

Old Saying

I'm like my grandmother. She was on the positive side whatever the situation. I'm for understanding and always there for people like she was.

Keana Bonds

[Grandmother] left no physical trace of her presence other than a silver mirror, a prayer book with mother-of-pearl covers, and a fistful of wax orange blossoms, remnants of her bridal headdress. . . . I heard people talk about her, and I hoard her few remaining relics in a tin box. All the rest I have invented, because we all need a grandmother.

Isabel Allende,
Paula

She had said on many occasions that I was impossible. And no matter how hard I tried, I could not live up to that woman's standards. She was impossible, too, which was her charm for me.

Ellen Gilchrist

$\mathcal{I}$ adored Grandma. . . . The songs she sang as she rocked me to sleep praised work and nature and told of the freedom that would someday come.

Josephine Baker

$\mathcal{B}$oth matriarchs, Judy and Julia, had graduated from college while neither of their husbands had. It impresses me that both of my grandfathers married women with brains, women who sought an education when it was not required or, in some cases even considered attractive.

Brett Butler

$\mathcal{G}$randmommy Judd was the voice of the Judds, the matriarch who ran the family, similar in that way to my Great-Grandmother Cora Lee. Cora Lee Burton and Sally Ellen Judd had their names in the phone book, which was very unusual at that time. Their husbands deferred to them.

Naomi Judd

My grandmother had no use for whiners. Her constant theme was, what you're supposed to do when you don't like a thing is change it. If you can't change it, change the way you think about it. Don't complain. It is said that persons have few teachable moments in their lives. Mamma seemed to have caught me at each one I had between the ages of three and thirteen.

       Maya Angelou

My great-grandfather used to say to his wife, my great-grandmother, who in turn told her daughter, my grandmother, who repeated it to her daughter, my mother, who used to remind her daughter, my own sister, that to talk well and eloquently was a very great art, but that an equally great one was to know the right moment to stop.

       Wolfgang Amadeus Mozart

My grandmother wanted to live long enough to vote for a woman president. I'll be satisfied if I live to see a woman go before the Supreme Court and hear the justices acknowledge, "Gentlemen, she's human. She deserves the protection of our laws."
      Martha Wright Griffiths

In the years since I began following the ways of my grandmothers I have come to value the teachings, stories, and daily examples of living which they shared with me. I pity the younger girls of the future who will miss out on meeting some of these fine old women.

      Beverly Hungry Wolf

My Grandma told me once that life was just a patchwork quilt, of births and deaths and marriages and things, and sometimes when you're looking for a lovely piece of red you can find a knot of faded strings.
      Natalie Whitted Price

[My grandmother] was the anchor that kept our extended family together—she represented the history of our family's emigration from Mexico, and she was the source of and inspiration for the values we hold today. For me, she remains one of the fundamental influences in my life.

Andrea Arredondo Raya

To this day, I attribute my own sense of civic duty, family, and love of country to my grandmother and my mother. Whenever I worry that perhaps what is occurring today with politics and society is a harbinger of bad times, I think of my grandmother's constant faith and optimism, and I recall how difficult her life was, yet how much she enjoyed the simple things in life, and how she never lost hope that faith and charity would overcome all obstacles.

Fernando M. Torres-Gil

[My mother's mother], Gram McKoy, was a small, lovely woman whose English wedded African cadence to British inflection, the sound of which is still music to my soul.
      Colin L. Powell

My grandma won't be called Grandma or Granny. She says it makes her feel old. So we call her Sylvia.
      Mary Hoffman

The Best Club in the World

To "Grandma Anne,"

    I know you don't expect this note from an "in-law" but, after all, we are both members of the best club in the world—grandmotherhood. Isn't it marvelous?

    We get to enjoy all the good times and then—guess what!—we can go home at the end of the day. We tell tall stories, make scrumptious cookies, have lots of time to spend, and never come over empty-handed. It's great fun to spoil a grandchild.

    Our children have done a wonderful job raising little Jamie. He's really growing up so fast. Too fast, in my opinion. What will we do when he's grown? I guess we can only wait and see what it's like being great-grandmothers!

                          Your counterpart,
                            "Grandma Josephine"

What makes you coo in public, travel thousands of miles just to spend a weekend baby-sitting, weigh your wallet down with cute snapshots, and simply feel terrific? A grandchild of course!
Audrey Sherins and Joan Holleman,
The Joy of Grandparenting

Grandmothers of long standing speak of it as a second chance. They remember the dreadful mistakes they made, or think they made, as parents, and their grandchildren give them the opportunity to recreate themselves in a more satisfying parental image.
Ruth Goode

Being a grandparent has all the joys of parenting without the sleepless nights.
Selma Wasserman

If becoming a grandmother was only a matter of choice I should advise every one of you straight-away to become one. There is no fun for old people like it!
Hannah Whitall Smith

Our grandchildren, in their generous way, have given us back those childhood moments, reconnecting us to our senses.
Gloria Gaither

Being a grandmother is always an adventure!
Helen Gurvitch

The day you were born
All my dreams came true
I'm the proudest Grandmother
To have a Grandchild like you.

Anonymous

Being a grandmother doesn't make me feel old. It makes me feel enriched. It is one of the most incredible experiences of my life.

Anonymous

I don't know about you, but I love the things my granddaughter can make herself and I know of only one way to convince her that the things we make have far more love in them than anything we can buy. . . . Even though I am a really lousy knitter and crocheter, I will make a hat and scarf for that doll [I bought her] . . . and my granddaughter will know that there was more love in that effort than in paying for the doll. She may not use the hat and scarf, and she may not be crazy about my handiwork, but she will be quite certain about the love.

Eda LeShan

Being a grandmother is the icing on the cake!
        Eleanor Budoff

It's a very practical house. It has a whole wing for the grandchildren.
        Angela Lansbury

Life is such a miracle, such a wonder, that no scientific advances can explain away its glory. And we grandmothers are, of all creatures, most blessed because we now have the time, the perspective, and the experience to "pay attention" to this amazing wonder.
        Gloria Gaither

Spoil them, love them, indulge them, then send them back to their parents to civilize them again.
        Joan McIntosh

I've decided to order some business cards for my daughter. I'm considering ordering a set for me: GRANDMOTHER. I'd be proud carrying them. Grandmothering is a full time love occupation.
Margaret Anne Huffman

"*H*ey, Mom," says the voice on the other end of the line. "What are you doing the week of the 14th?" "Send the child" is my response. "Whatever I'm doing, I'll cancel."
Rolaine Hochstein

*A*s a grandmother, I am learning more about children than I did from raising my own. I keep all the cards, pictures, and school papers my grandchildren send me. Sometimes I wish I could have been a grandmother before being a mother. It would have helped me be more understanding and forgiving.
Betty Steele Everett

$\mathcal{M}$aria and Margaret, my oldest daughter, could have had a nanny, but they wanted [me] their mother, which I thought, and still think, was wonderful.

Matilda Raffa Cuomo

$\mathcal{I}$f a grandmother wants to put her foot down, the only safe place to do it these days is in a notebook.

Florida Scott-Maxwell

$\mathcal{T}$he best face lift is the smile your grandchild puts on your face.

Anonymous

$\mathcal{I}$'m typical in every way as a grandmother, though I haven't gotten around to baking cookies yet.

Chaka Khan

The best things you can give to your grandchildren are love and time. . . . The great reward of being a grandparent is that your grandchild, like your mother and father, loves you for yourself—and for no other reason.

       T. Berry Brazelton, M.D.

You don't travel empty-handed. You bring gifts. (Sometimes the gifts even travel without you.) Whenever I go into a store these days, something pulls me to the children's department. It's my husband.

       Rolaine Hochstein

Being a grandmother is like being part of the best club in the world.

       Mary Liporulo

"Grandma" from Around the World

Chinese	*	*Zu-mu*
Dutch	*	*Grootmoeder*
French	*	*Grandmère*
German	*	*Oma*
Hebrew	*	*Savta*
Italian	*	*Nonna*
Japanese	*	*Obaa-San*
Russian	*	*Babushka*
Spanish	*	*Abuela*
Zulu	*	*Gogo*